ALIENS

You are not of this world

BY
CHAD GONZALES

ALIENS – You Are Not of This World
ISBN 13: 978-0-9777380-5-2
Copyright © 2011, 2014 by Chad W. Gonzales

TABLE OF CONTENTS

TABLE OF CONTENTS

Introduction

Growing up in the eighties in a Christian home, I was forced to listen to the Christian music of that day. Now to be honest, most of the Christian music in the eighties didn't leave much to be desired; I don't think I would be too off based in saying that most of it was pretty bland.

I've always been a musician at heart and loved music, but there wasn't much Christian music I really wanted to listen to back then. However, there were two groups I thoroughly enjoyed listening to: Mylon LeFevre and Broken Heart and another group called Petra. In my opinion, both of these groups paved the way for modern Christian music - and satisfied my need for some good music!

I'll never forget one song Petra released called "Not Of This World" written by Bob Hartman. Back then, I never really paid much attention to the words, but for some reason, the words of that song resonated with me over the years. A few months back, the words of this song started echoing in my mind and it began the journey in which I am about to take you. Here are the lyrics:

We are Pilgrims in a strange land
We are so far from our homeland
With each passing day it seems so clear
This world will never want us here
We're not welcome in this world of wrong
We are foreigners who don't belong
We are strangers, we are aliens
We are not of this world
We are envoys we must tarry
With this message we must carry
There's so much to do before we leave
With so many more who may believe
Our mission here can never fail
And the gates of hell will not prevail
Jesus told us men would hate us
But we must be of good cheer
He has overcome this world of darkness
And we will soon depart from here

For days, those words "We are strangers, we are aliens, we are not of this world" continued to replay in my mind. It was during that time I read a passage of scripture I had read many times, but this time, it really penetrated my heart.

In John 8:23, Jesus said, "I am from above, you are from beneath. You are of this world; I am not of this world." I began to really feel a tug on the inside that I needed to study this more. As I began to read the book of John, the magnitude of this reality began to rock my world.

I am a hardcore believer in the importance of
you are in Christ. Over the years, I have spent
studying and ministering in this area, but I had
the importance of this piece of our identity as b
origin. When I began to see how much importance Jesus
placed on it, then I knew it must be important.
I began to see how this reality of Heaven played a key role in
walking in power, manifesting God's power, ministering in
strong faith, ushering in the last day revival and absolutely
demolishing all hell could bring my way.

I want to share these truths with you and help you know
with certainty, that just like Jesus, you are not of this world.
I guarantee it will revolutionize your thinking and thus
revolutionize your life!

CHAPTER ONE
JESUS WAS AN ALIEN

And He said to them, "You are from beneath; I am
from above. You are of this world; I am not of this
world."
John 8:23 NKJV

Within this statement, Jesus gives us so much information
as to the success of His life and ministry on the earth. We
can see His thoughts, His meditations and tremendous keys
as to how He was able to do all that He did.

One of the foundational keys to Jesus' success is found in
this one word: ORIGIN. The word origin means: the point
at which something begins its course or existence. Jesus
knew His origin; Jesus knew where He was from.

You see Jesus refer to His origin a number of times
throughout the Gospels. He would repeatedly tell people
where He was from; yet, it's interesting that we don't hear
Him talk of His natural birthplace or hometown; Jesus was

always speaking of His spiritual origin. He always told people He was from Heaven. Jesus was always speaking of Heaven; He constantly talked about where He was from and where He was going. If He was always talking about it, then He was always thinking about it and this was key to His identity and ultimately His success on the earth.

Your identity is largely comprised of your place of origin, citizenship, race and ethnicity. Where you are from, the culture you are born into, the language of that culture and the customs of that place play a tremendous role in shaping who you are. Where you are from has such a huge impact on your identity that it also plays a role in determining your self esteem, habits, life goals, etc. In many ways, we are very much products of our own environment.

Think about someone from a third world country compared to someone from the United States. Don't you think their goals and dreams would be quite different? The reason is that those from the third world country don't have the options available to them as opposed to the one from the United States. There are greater limitations and challenges for the person from the third world country as opposed to the American and therefore, these affect the outlooks and perspectives on life.

In the same manner, Jesus' knowledge of His origin tremendously affected His outlook on life while on the earth. Let's take a look at some of the statements Jesus made concerning His place of origin.

> And yet no one has ever gone up to heaven, but there
> is One Who has come down from heaven--the Son
> of Man [Himself], Who is (dwells, has His home) in
> heaven.
> John 3:13 AMP

This is absolutely one of my favorite scriptures in the
Bible. Jesus is talking to Nicodemus and explaining the
importance of salvation and being born again. Then Jesus
makes this eye popping, mind bending statement: "I'm from
heaven and heaven is where I am right now."

Notice where Jesus said He was from. He didn't say
Bethlehem or Nazareth; Jesus said He was from Heaven.
Heaven was His place of origin; Heaven was His home.
Secondly, notice that latter phrase, "...the Son of Man who
is in heaven." It's a staggering statement with mind blowing
truths for you and I and one which we will look further into
in a later chapter.

> For God so loved the world that He gave His only
> begotten Son, that whoever believes in Him should
> not perish but have everlasting life. God did not
> send His Son into the world to condemn the world
> but to save it.
> John 3:16, 17 NKJV

After making this staggering statement in John 3:13, we
come to a passage of scripture most people are aware of:

John 3:16, 17. Notice again, Jesus states that He isn't from earth; He was sent here. For Jesus to be sent into the world, it means He had to come from another world. *You can't go into something you are already in; you have to be outside of something to go into it.* Most of us have a pretty firm understanding that Jesus was from Heaven; yet again, the key is that Jesus had to understand He was from Heaven. Jesus knew Heaven was His home.

> **Jesus answered and said to them, "Even if I bear witness of Myself, My witness is true, for I know where I came from and where I am going; but you do not know where I come from and where I am going." And He said to them, "You are from beneath; I am from above. You are of this world; I am not of this world."**
> **John 8:14, 23 NKJV**

Again, Jesus plainly states to the religious people of the day that earth is not His home. I love the boldness in which Jesus spoke the truth. He essentially told them, "You are from hell; I am from Heaven." Can you imagine telling someone that? Yet, this is what Jesus said.

I guarantee you that many people who preach Jesus today would have been offended by Him when He walked the earth. Jesus didn't sugar coat anything; He told it like it was. Many Christians today would accuse Jesus of not being loving and accepting and being too brash. Let me tell you something friend, Jesus spoke the truth. True love speaks the truth! Jesus sat right there and told the religious leaders to their face that they were of hell and the devil was their daddy!

Jesus went on to further establish His point by saying He was not of this world. Jesus was very much conscious of where He was from; the reality of His home in Heaven was greater than the reality of His home on the earth.

It's interesting to note how many times Jesus refers to Himself as being sent from Heaven. Just in the Gospel of John, Jesus refers to Himself as being sent from Heaven seventeen times. Seventeen! If Jesus continually said something, then it probably carried an extreme amount of importance for Him and for us.

> And Jesus said, "For judgment I have come into this world, that those who do not see may see, and that those who see may be made blind."
> John 9:39 NKJV

Again, Jesus tells us that He came into the world; notice He also knew He came with something to give!

> I have come as a light into the world, that whoever believes in Me should not abide in darkness.
> John 12:46 NKJV

As in John 9:39, Jesus states plainly that He not only came

into this world, but He also came with a purpose along with equipment to fulfill that purpose.

> **Jesus answered, "My kingdom is not of this world. If My kingdom were of this world, My servants would fight, so that I should not be delivered to the Jews; but now My kingdom is not from here."**
> John 18:36 NKJV

This last scripture is very important. Not only do we see that Jesus understood His origin and His purpose, we also see that Jesus understood He was the head of a kingdom. This kingdom did not have its origin in the earth; it was a kingdom from another world. Jesus very bluntly states, "My kingdom is not from here." We will also look at this truth in greater detail in another chapter.

We must understand why it was so important that Jesus understood where He was from; it's crucial that Jesus understood this because if He didn't, it would have hindered Him in fulfilling God's plan for His life. Remember, seventeen times Jesus refers to His heavenly origin. This was an extremely important truth for Him; therefore, it is an extremely important truth for you and I.

Chapter Two
We Are Not Of This World

They are not of the world, just as I am not of the world.
John 17:16 NKJV

You may be saying, "Well, that's fine and all. I know that Jesus was from Heaven and I understand that Jesus knew He was from Heaven - but what does this mean for me?"

Well, did you see what Jesus said? Just like Jesus, as a believer, you are not of this world. There are two important words in that scripture that really stand out to me: just as. This phrase means: "of the very same quality; to the very same degree; in precisely the very same way." Jesus just flat out told you that Heaven is your home! Want more proof? Look at the rest of Jesus' prayer in John 17.

Now I am no longer in the world, but these are in the world, and I come to You. Holy Father, keep through Your name those whom You have given

Me, that they may be one as We are. While I was with them in the world, I kept them in Your name. I have given them
Your word; and the world has hated them because they are not of the world, just as I am not of the world. I do not pray that You should take them out of the world, but that You should keep them from the evil one. They are not of the world, just as I am not of the world. Sanctify them by Your truth. Your word is truth. As You sent Me into the world, I also have sent them into the world.
John 17:11-18 NKJV

In every verse except for verse 13 and 17, Jesus states in one way or another that you are an alien from another world. Notice Jesus continually says that you are in the world and it is in the context of it being temporary just as His time in the world. He also states that just as He was sent into the world, He has sent us into the world. We will also explore this truth later as well.

If you were of the world, the world would love its own. Yet because you are not of the world, but I chose you out of the world, therefore the world hates you.
John 15:19 NKJV

Again, this is Jesus talking. Did you see what He said about you? Here is more proof from the mouth of Jesus Christ that you are not from here. What you experience with your five senses is not your home and not your place of origin.

We literally are not from here. You may have been born in the earth, but it's not where you are from. You see, when you accepted Jesus Christ as your Lord and Savior, 2 Corinthians 5:17 says that you became a brand new creature. The old you passed away and a brand new you was born. When you received salvation, you became brand new with a brand new origin.

You have to understand that you are a spirit being; the real you is not what you see in the mirror - that is just your physical house for your spirit. The Bible plainly tells us that we are a triune being, a three part being (1 Thessalonians 5:23). We are a spirit, we have a soul (our mind, will and emotions) and we have a body. When you accepted salvation, your spirit became brand new, yet the mind you think with and the body you walk with stayed the same. This is why the apostle Paul made statements like "renew your mind" and "crucify your flesh." Why? Because those two pieces weren't saved; they were not made new like your spirit.

A Citizen of Heaven

Just like with your natural citizenship, your spiritual citizenship occurs the same way: by birth. If you were born in the United States, then you are automatically a United States citizen; the same holds true in the spiritual realm.

You may have been born in the United States, France,

Mexico, Australia, India or some other country, but it's not the origin of the true you. You are literally from another world with a temporary existence on this planet called earth.

Saved or unsaved, we are spirit beings with a spiritual origin. If you have never accepted salvation, then your home is hell. Some people may not like that, but it's not my opinion - it's Bible! If you have accepted salvation, then your home is Heaven. Citizenship is by birth. If your citizenship is in hell, then there is good news; you can change citizenships! Accept Jesus as your Lord and Savior and be born again! The doors of citizenship are always open and the stamp of the blood of Jesus forever seals that citizenship.

> **But our citizenship is in heaven. And we eagerly await a Savior from there, the Lord Jesus Christ. Philippians 3:20 NKJV**

So just like Jesus, Heaven is your home. It was extremely important for this to be a reality in His life and it's extremely important for it to be a reality in your life. Say it with me," Heaven is my home! It's where I am from and where I am going!"

Even those in the Old Testament had an understanding about this truth. People like King David and Abraham had a glimpse of truth in this area; they understood their time here on earth was just temporary. They understood they were aliens in this world and Heaven was their place of origin.

> **For we are aliens and pilgrims before You, As were all our fathers; Our days on earth are as a shadow, And without hope.**
> 1 Chronicles 29:15 NKJV

> **These people all died controlled and sustained by their faith, but not having received the tangible fulfillment of [God's] promises, only having seen it and greeted it from a great distance by faith, and all the while acknowledging and confessing that they were strangers and temporary residents and exiles upon the earth.**
> Hebrews 11:13 AMP

When we get a revelation of this marvelous truth, it will change our lives. Heaven is where I am from! "I am a supernatural being with a supernatural origin living in a natural world." This has to be your mindset. It has to be how you view yourself; otherwise, regardless of your heavenly origin, you will succumb to and be complacent in living a very natural ordinary life subject to the circumstances all around you.

You are in the world, but you are not of this world. You are from another planet. You are a different breed of being, a different species of life on planet earth. Your citizenship is in Heaven and you received it by birth!

Chapter Three
Conscious Of Another World

Jesus answered, "Even if I testify on my own behalf, my testimony is valid, for I know where I came from and where I am going. But you have no idea where I come from or where I am going."
John 8:14 NKJV

We are supernatural extraordinary beings who have become complacent with a natural ordinary life. Why? <u>Because we haven't been aware of our origin; we haven't been aware of our true identity.</u>

If you are not aware of something, then you can't use it. I remember one time I was looking through the console in my car and found a $20 bill folded up between some music CD's; I had forgotten that it was there. There were times I could have used that twenty dollars, but I couldn't use it because I was not conscious of the fact that I had it. In the same way, we can't live a life of Heaven if we aren't conscious of it. We can't live the way God intended for us after salvation if we don't know what we have!

Do you know one of the main differences between Jesus' life on the earth and our life on the earth? Jesus was conscious of another world. Jesus was aware of His origin from Heaven; He was aware of His kingdom; He was conscious of spiritual things.

It's sad, but most Christians today are ignorant of spiritual things; most of us have more trust and confidence in the things we can see and hear. We put more trust in a doctor's report or economist's report than God's Word. I like something Kenneth E. Hagin used to say, "Most Christians wouldn't recognize the Holy Spirit if He walked in the room wearing a red hat." We are spiritual, Heavenly beings made in the likeness and image of God and yet are dumb to who we really are and Whose we are. We need to become more conscious of God and things pertaining to the Spirit.

Fortunately for us, Jesus wasn't ignorant in His identity and origin. Jesus was very keenly aware of the world He was from. He not only knew He was from another world, He was conscious of that world.

The greater your awareness, the greater the benefits

There are some great benefits that come from being conscious of the other world you are from. First of all, it will break you free from natural limitations. The greater your consciousness of the Heavenly world you are from, the greater freedom you will see in your life.

Because Jesus was conscious of Heaven, He lived different. It affected His belief system, His language, thoughts, and actions; it permeated His entire way of living. His consciousness of this other world gave Him an unwavering confidence and boldness in His ministry on the earth.

> You judge me by human standards, but I do not judge anyone. And if I did, my judgment would be correct in every respect because I am not alone. The Father who sent me is with me. Your own law says that if two people agree about something, their witness is accepted as fact. I am one witness, and my Father who sent me is the other.
> John 8:15-18 NLT

For Jesus, the unseen was more real than the seen. Jesus relied more on the testimony of God that He didn't see than the testimony of man that He could see. To Jesus, God was more real to Him than the people standing in front of Him. Jesus was conscious of another world and also conscious of the God of that world. Jesus staked His life and ministry on the unseen world.

> You see, the realm of the spirit is very real, more real than the realm of the natural.
> By faith we understand that the worlds were framed by the word of God, so that the things which are seen were not made of things which are visible.
> Hebrews 11:3 NKJV

All of creation came from Someone and somewhere you don't see. It was created from another world; the same world we call home: Heaven. This is why Jesus wasn't shaken when it came to healing the sick or raising the dead or turning the water into wine. He was using something from the unseen world from which He was from to affect the seen world of which He was in.

The more aware you are of the other world, the bolder you will be to proclaim the truths of that world. You will stop putting up with and identifying with natural circumstances; instead, despite what you see, you will still identify with your Heavenly origin! Remember, you may be in the world, but you are not of the world. We don't have to live, act and talk like the world!

As we become more aware of our origin, we will stop being caught up with natural things.

People that struggle with sin in their lives aren't conscious of where they are from. Sinners sin; believers don't. Sinning is what people from this earthly world do; it's natural to them; it is part of their identity. As a citizen of Heaven, born in the likeness and image of God, a sinful lifestyle isn't part of my nature or identity. That junk doesn't go on where I am from! I am from Heaven and my focus is on Heavenly things.

> **Dear friends, I urge you, as foreigners and exiles, to abstain from sinful desires, which wage war against your soul.**
> **1 Peter 2:11 NKJV**

The more conscious you are of Heaven, the stronger you will be in your stance when negative circumstances arise. You won't back down!

> **All these people were still living by faith when they died. They did not receive the things promised; they only saw them and welcomed them from a distance, admitting that they were foreigners and strangers on earth. People who say such things show that they are looking for a country of their own. If they had been thinking of the country they had left, they would have had opportunity to return. Instead, they were longing for a better country—a heavenly one.**
> **Hebrews 11:13-16 NKJV**

Notice they weren't thinking of their natural origin; they were thinking of their Heavenly origin. They had their focus on where they were going back to: Heaven! You see, when times are tough and your focus is on natural things, you will always resort to natural solutions and natural reactions. Yet when it's crunch time and your focus is on Heaven, you will never look back or look down. You will look straight ahead with your feet anchored in the ground immovable, unshakeable and full of glory! Your consciousness of the other world will sustain you.

> **Do not conform to the pattern of this world, but be transformed by the renewing of your mind.**
> **Romans 12:2 NKJV**

You see, we shouldn't be living like the world. We aren't like them. I don't mean that in a condescending way, but we aren't. We are different. We've been born out of Heaven, cleansed by the blood of Christ and made righteous! God doesn't want us conforming to the way of living in the world. Unfortunately, most Christians live like the world not only in actions, but also in their marriage, finances, health, etc. Why? Because they haven't renewed their mind to the truths of God's Word. Most of us haven't renewed our mind to the truth that Heaven is really our home.

Chapter Four
A Foreign Mindset

Do not be conformed to this world (this age),
[fashioned after and adapted to its external,
superficial customs], but be transformed (changed)
by the [entire] renewal of your mind [by its new
ideals and its new attitude], so that you may prove
[for yourselves] what is the good and acceptable and
perfect will of God, even the thing which is good
and acceptable and perfect [in His sight for you].
Romans 12:2 AMP

If we want to see the truths of what we have previously
looked at transform our lives, then we must transform our
thinking. The greatest limiter in your life is your mind.
Even though you may be saved, if you still think like the
world, you will act like the world, talk like the world, smell
like the world and have results like the world. Remember
what I told you earlier? When you received salvation, your
spirit was born again, but not your soul or body.

Notice that you being conformed to this world has everything to do with your mind. Have you ever known someone who moved to your country from another country? Did you notice that after a while, they started to talk and act differently? After being in the new country for many years, they began to take on the cultural norms of the new country. They started talking different, dressing different, eating different, etc. Why? Because they started thinking like those in the new country and therefore began adapting to the culture and lifestyle.

When our mother gave birth to us in that hospital room, we began a journey of learning the culture and lifestyle of this present world. After many years, we became extremely adapted to it and were just like everyone else. Then one day, you accepted Jesus as your Lord and Savior and were born again; you became a brand new creature from Heaven - and yet still stuck with the same mind and same body. Now for you to see a difference, you have to start thinking like the country you are from: Heaven.

This is why the apostle Paul tells us to renew our mind. We must start thinking like someone from another world; we must begin thinking like someone from Heaven!

> **Dear friends, I warn you as "temporary residents and foreigners" to keep away from worldly desires that wage war against your very souls.**
> **1 Peter 2:11 NLT**

I'm not saying it's easy, because it's not; this is one of the greatest trials for the believer. Everything you see, hear, smell, taste and touch tells you that you are natural and you are limited. Everything around you tells you that you are the same after you were saved than before you were saved. When you look in the mirror, there is nothing that says, "Hey, you aren't from here!" This is where God's Word is so important. The Word of God is like a spiritual mirror that you can look into and see what you are truly like. The more you look in that mirror, the more you will understand what God made you to be!

Let this mind be in you

I've said it for years and I'll keep saying it: If you want to do what Jesus did, then you must think like Jesus thought. One thing many of us forget about is that Jesus, although the Son of God, walked this earth as a Man. Jesus never talked about his natural origins, but throughout the Gospels, we are told several times about His manhood.

> **Let this mind be in you which was also in Christ Jesus, who, being in the form of God, did not consider it robbery to be equal with God, but made Himself of no reputation, taking the form of a bondservant, and coming in the likeness of men.
> Philippians 2:5-7 NKJV**

You must understand that Jesus walked this earth just like you and I. He didn't have any greater privileges or equipment than you and I have as a child of God. The Bible says that He laid aside His advantages as God and came to this earth as a Man. This is why Jesus could be our High Priest because He experienced everything that we experience in this natural world.

> **For we do not have a high priest who is unable to empathize with our weaknesses, but we have one who has been tempted in every way, just as we are—yet he did not sin.**
> Hebrews 4:15 NIV

Jesus had a mind problem just like you and I; He had to constantly keep His thoughts on Heavenly things. Friend, the more you think about Heaven and talk about Heaven, the more of Heaven you will experience in your life. This was so crucial to Jesus' life and ministry.

Jesus was from Heaven but was naturally born in this earth. Jesus had to grow in His revelation and understanding of His Heavenly origin just like you and I.

> **There the child grew strong in body and wise in spirit. And the grace of God was on him.**
> Luke 2:40 MSG

From the very beginning of His earthly life, Jesus was growing in His understanding of who He truly was and where He was from. Luke 2:40 isn't talking about Jesus learning His A-B-C's and 1-2-3's; Jesus grew in Godly wisdom and spiritual things.

As Jesus grew in the revelation of who He truly was, it began to affect the world around Him. Jesus began to see victory and domination in every area of life because He knew where He was from.

Revelation is progressive and takes time. You see this progression even in Jesus' life. Take for example Jesus' confidence in the supernatural. Without a doubt, Jesus was a master at operating in the power of God, but in the beginning of His ministry, you see Jesus taking steps in His identity and steps in domination of natural things.

Take for example Jesus and His mastery of water. He started out turning water into wine, then He calmed the sea and later walked on the sea. Do you see the progression of dominance?

Consider Jesus and the three miracles of raising people from the dead. The first person Jesus raised from the dead was Jairus' daughter; she had only been dead a few hours. The second person Jesus raised from the dead was the widow woman's son; he had been dead about a day. Jesus raised Him up during the funeral procession! The third person we see Jesus raise up was Lazarus. We know according to scripture that Lazarus had been dead for four days. Lazarus had already been laid in the tomb! Again you see Jesus go from one degree to another degree of mastery.

By the way, have you ever wondered why Jesus waited four days to raise up Lazarus? After all, He waited two more days from the day he found out Lazarus was dead.

> **So when Jesus came, He found that he had already been in the tomb four days. Now Bethany was near Jerusalem, about two miles away.**
> **John 11:17-18 NKJV**

I think it's interesting that we are told Jesus was only two miles away. Don't you see what was happening here? Jesus was using this for training! He was using this to stretch Himself for complete and total domination of death. Jesus arrived four days after Lazarus had died. Why? Buckle your seat belt and hold on for this one: Jesus knew if He could raise Lazarus up in four days, He could raise Himself up in three days! Glory to God! Jesus was a faith man; but, operating on this earth as a man, He had to continually renew His mind and stretch His imagination and the working of His faith just like you and I.

You see, the more you think like Heaven, the more of Heaven you will manifest. Remember the statement Jesus made in John 3:13? "Heaven is where I am from, Heaven is where I am going and Heaven is where I am now." Jesus was operating out of Heaven because He had his mind on Heavenly things.

Like I said earlier, everything around you is screaming limits! Yet, for a born again believer in Christ, the only limit in your life is your mind.

> Now to Him who is able to do exceedingly abundantly above all that we ask or think, according to the power that works in us.
> Ephesians 3:20 NKJV

This verse tells us that the power released is according to the degree of which you will allow yourself to think and speak. We've been thinking and speaking like earthlings for too long! I know that sounds funny, but it's true. We need to start thinking and speaking like aliens from Heaven!

In Heaven, there is no sickness and disease. In Heaven, there is no weakness, death, depression, addictions, poverty, or lack. Get this in your head! Heaven is where you are from. That is the society of which you were born into. It should be what we are accustomed to; therefore, it should be engrained into our souls! Just because things around us don't look like Heaven doesn't mean it has to affect you. But earthly circumstances will affect you if you don't get your thoughts and words lined up with Heaven. You will have what you say.

> *Jesus didn't allow earthly circumstances to change His thoughts and speech.*

Then he said, "Our friend Lazarus has fallen asleep, but now I will go and wake him up." The disciples said, "Lord, if he is sleeping, he will soon get better!"

> They thought Jesus meant Lazarus was simply sleeping, but Jesus meant Lazarus had died. So he told them plainly, "Lazarus is dead. And for your sakes, I'm glad I wasn't there, for now you will really believe. Come, let's go see him."
> John 11:11-15 NLT

Notice Jesus isn't speaking according to earthly fact; Jesus was speaking about things according to Heaven. The disciples just didn't get it so Jesus had to come down on their level, an earthly level, and explain things according to Heavenly standards.

Thinking like an earthling will limit you. Even though Heaven is where you are from, if you don't think like that and talk like that, you will live just like every other human being on this planet. I'm not necessarily saying you need to tell everyone you come into contact with that you are from another planet - they might try to have you committed to a psychiatric ward - but you need to meditate on these things.

Think like a foreigner. Think back to the way things are in Heaven. Imagine yourself there and think about what it is like. Imagine what would happen if you were in Heaven and confronted with the same problems you are confronted with on earth?

How would you handle it? How would it affect you? How would you think about that situation? How you would think about it in Heaven is the way you should think about it on earth.

Set It and Forget It

And now, dear brothers and sisters, one final thing. Fix your thoughts on what is true, and honorable, and right, and pure, and lovely, and admirable. Think about things that are excellent and worthy of praise. Keep putting into practice all you learned and received from me—everything you heard from me and saw me doing. Then the God of peace will be with you.
Philippians 4:8-9 NLT

In this life, you will be faced with some very negative circumstances. In those times, your mind needs to be fixed on the things of Heaven. Your mind needs to be set on the way things operate in Heaven. We were designed to live on this earth and yet live like we are in Heaven with no limitations and no lack or need. Yet, too many times we allow our minds to wander from Heaven's answers to earth's problems.

I'm reminded of this infomercial that used to come on late night television for this particular rotisserie machine. Their marketing slogan was "Set it and forget it." The main selling point of this machine was the ease of which it operated; you just set the timer, put in your chicken and walked away. I've never forgotten that slogan because it held so much truth for me as a believer. When the trials and tests of life come your way, you take your thoughts, set them on the things of Heaven, forget the circumstances and walk away.

Jesus didn't spend time meditating on the problems of life. Jesus meditated on the solutions of Heaven. Jesus spent time thinking about His homeland and the way things were supposed to be; He stretched His imaginations regarding the solutions, not the dilemmas. If you want to have the earthly success of Jesus, you need to think like He thought.

CHAPTER FIVE
A FOREIGN LANGUAGE

God...calls those things which do not exist as though they did.
Romans 4:17 NKJV

Have you ever been around someone speaking a foreign language? It sounds a little funny doesn't it? Unless you speak that same language, it just doesn't register with your brain. If you began speaking to someone and they responded in a foreign language you didn't understand, you would think they might be a odd.

Every country has an official language. If you are in that country, you are expected to speak that language. If you went to Mexico and started speaking Swahili, they would look at you pretty strange. Why? Well, simply because that language doesn't match up with that country. People expect you to speak the language of the country. If you don't, they aren't going to understand you and may even get a little upset!

Heaven is a country; it is a kingdom and land all of its own. Heaven is comparable to no other country which has ever been on planet earth; the only place on earth that ever came close was the Garden of Eden. It was Heaven on earth - at least until Adam sinned.

Heaven not only has it's own culture and different ways of doing things, it also has an official language. It's called the language of Faith (Romans 10:8). This language doesn't make sense to the natural mind because it goes absolutely contrary to natural circumstances. You see, it doesn't follow the same rules that other languages do. For example, Faith doesn't have a past or future tense; Faith only allows for the present.

> **Now faith is confidence in what we hope for (expect right now) and assurance about what we do not see.**
> Hebrews 11:1 NIV
> **(Parenthesis are author's notes)**

NOW FAITH! It's not later faith; it's now. Faith doesn't necessarily talk about what God is going to do; faith talks about what God has already done and therefore what is mine right now.

Faith doesn't allow for things to be placed in the future because the Author of this language doesn't live in the future. God always lives in the now! Faith is based on what God has already done, never on what God is going to do. God has already accomplished and has already provided everything you will ever need on this earth.

Faith isn't a language made up of vowels and consonants; it's a language of perspective. It is speaking things the way God sees them - not the way that earth sees them. Honestly, on the earth, there are truly only two languages spoken: Faith or Fear. The language of Faith is based on the rule of "Call it like God sees it." The language of Fear is based on the rule of "Call it like I see it." Faith says what it needs to be; Fear says what it is.

For most earthlings, the language of Faith is the strangest language they have ever heard. If you start speaking Faith, most people will think you are an outright crazy looney tune. Why? Because Faith demands for you to call things differently than the way you see them with your physical eyes. It's not about what I see on the earth; it's about what I see in Heaven. I call things the way it is in Heaven!

> God...calls those things which do not exist as though they did.
> Romans 4:17 NKJV

If my body is sick, I have a choice. I can speak the language of "call it like I see it" or "call it like God sees it." As an alien on this planet, I have to make a choice. Am I going to think and talk like an earthling or am I going to think and talk like an alien from Heaven? If I am to talk like an earthling, then I will agree with my body, speak the language of Fear and say, "I feel horrible." If I decide to act like a citizen of

Heaven, then I will line up my thoughts and words with the ways of Heaven, speak the language of Faith and say, "According to 1 Peter 2:24, By His stripes, I am healed. I call my body healed and whole from the top of my head to the soles of my feet!"

If my finances take a nosedive, I can get fearful and start crying like someone who isn't from Heaven or I can remember where I am from and start declaring that "According to Philippians 4:19, all my needs are met and all my bills are paid!"

The language of Faith doesn't call it like it is; Faith calls it the way it needs to be! That's what God does and that is what Jesus did on the earth. Remember the story of Lazarus?

> These things He said, and after that He said to them, "Our friend Lazarus sleeps, but I go that I may wake him up." Then His disciples said, "Lord, if he sleeps he will get well." However, Jesus spoke of his death, but they thought that He was speaking about taking rest in sleep. Then Jesus said to them plainly, "Lazarus is dead. And I am glad for your sakes that I was not there, that you may believe. Nevertheless let us go to him."
> John 11:11-15 NKJV

Jesus was speaking Faith and the disciples didn't understand the language. This wasn't the first time that people didn't understand Jesus. Look at the story of Jairus' daughter.

> **While Jesus was still speaking, some people came
> from the house of Jairus, the synagogue leader.
> "Your daughter is dead," they said. "Why bother
> the teacher anymore?"   Overhearing what they
> said, Jesus told him, "Don't be afraid; just believe."
> He did not let anyone follow him except Peter,
> James and John the brother of James. When they
> came to the home of the synagogue leader, Jesus
> saw a commotion, with people crying and wailing
> loudly. He went in and said to them, "Why all this
> commotion and wailing? The child is not dead but
> asleep." But they laughed at him.**
> Mark 5:35-40 NIV

Again, you have two different perspectives and thus two
different languages. Jesus was speaking the language of
Faith; Jesus was conscious of His homeland. Everyone
else was speaking the language of Fear because they were
conscious of their present circumstances and the limitations
of their homeland.

Do you see this?   This language and perspective was foreign
to these people. They not only didn't understand it, but
they laughed at Jesus and mocked Him. Don't be surprised
when your family and friends laugh at you - and don't be
surprised if they are Christians.

Sadly, Faith is a funny language even to most of the
Christian world because the people born of Heaven don't

even realize it. Their perspective is not from Heaven so they naturally have a natural perspective. Faith calls those things that be not as though they are; Faith calls it the way you see it in Heaven, not the way you see it on earth.

When you are driving a beat up car with duct tape on the tires and you start talking about how you are rich - don't be surprised when people start asking if you need some psychotropic drugs. When everyone knows the doctor gave you a death sentence and you start talking about how healed you are and the plans you have fifty years from now - don't be surprised when people try to get you to see a therapist. You see, earthlings want you to get a grip on their reality! What they don't understand is you do have a grip on reality. The fact may be that you are broke, but the truth of the matter is that you have a Heavenly bank account they can't see; in that bank account is all the riches of Heaven at your disposal!

I don't care what people think about me or say about me. They aren't standing in my shoes and experiencing my circumstances. They may see my finances, my health, my business or any other facet of my life as dead. They can laugh all they want, they can jeer all they want and they can criticize all they want. They can say whatever they want, but I will keep speaking the language of Heaven. I speak Faith and I call every area of my life ALIVE! I always have what I say!

CHAPTER SIX
SUPERPOWERS

We now have this light shining in our hearts, but we ourselves are like fragile clay jars containing this great treasure. This makes it clear that our great power is from God, not from ourselves.
2 Corinthians 4:7 NLT

I don't know about you, but I've never seen a movie where the aliens were less powerful than the people of earth. Movie after movie, you always see the same thing: the aliens invade earth with extraordinary capabilities, machinery, technology and powers. Even one of the most popular superheroes of all time was a man called Clark Kent, aka Superman. The story of Superman and other such stories truly have a great deal of their inspiration from the Bible - although the writers of these stories may not have realized it.

From the beginning of time, human nature has always been obsessed with the supernatural and has always looked for ways to tap into a supernatural power. Do you know why?

It's plain and simple: man was created for it.

When God created man, He made human beings in His very image and likeness (Gen 1:27). God made man in His very own class. Man was distinct from all the other creatures God made. Man wasn't made with four legs and a tail, man wasn't given fins or feathers and man wasn't made to be an angel. Man was made with the ability to fellowship with God on His level and operate just like God on the earth.

The treasure of God's creation was created to operate like Him and Jesus proved it to be so. Jesus showed us through His earthly ministry the standard of living available to God's children. Jesus showed us what a man full of faith and full of the Holy Spirit was supposed to look like; Jesus was our example.

The Gospels in many respects read like a Superman story. Here is this Man named Jesus from another planet. He turns water into wine, raises the dead, causes the blind to see, the deaf to hear and the lame to walk. He feeds over five thousand people with only five loaves of bread and two fish - twice.

He speaks to trees and they die. He speaks to the wind and it stops. When people are sinking in water, Jesus is walking on it. Every time His enemies try to capture Him, He's untouchable. Hundreds of soldiers try to capture Him,

Jesus says two words and the whole army falls flat to the ground. His story culminates with not only dominating the physical realm, but also dominating the spiritual realm and rising from the dead. Wow! And He did it without any special costume!

Again, most people, including Christians will say, "Yeah, but that was Jesus. He was different. He was the Son of God." Well, it is true that He was different and He was the Son of God. He was different because until then, He was the only human being ever on the planet since Adam and Eve that was full of the life and nature of God.

Now let me ask you a question? As a believer with Jesus as your Lord and Savior, are you not full of the life and nature of God? Yes you are. Let me ask you a second question. As a believer with Jesus as your Lord and Savior, are you not also a child of God? Yes you are.

You also have to remember that Jesus repeatedly told people the power wasn't His power and He, in and of Himself, could not do the miraculous. Now I know that goes against a whole lot of religion, but it's plain and simple Bible.

I can of Myself do nothing.
John 5:30 NKJV

Do you not believe that I am in the Father, and the Father in Me? The words that I speak to you I do not speak on My own authority; but the Father who

dwells in Me does the works.
John 14:10 NKJV

Jesus was operating as a man anointed by God (Acts 10:38).
Yes, He was the Son of God, but He stripped Himself of
everything that would give Himself an advantage and came
to the earth as a man. Jesus also knew that He was sent on
a mission and that He had power to back up His words and
fulfill the mission.

Just like Jesus, we have been sent on a mission from Heaven
and we've been given the power of Heaven to fulfill all God
has called us to do. God didn't send you without some
weaponry and some proof of who you are!

As you sit there and think about that, let's go to one of my
all time favorite scriptures in the Bible.

I tell you the truth, anyone who believes in me will
do the same works I have done, and even greater
works, because I am going to be with the Father.
John 14:12 NLT

It's a staggering statement to our natural minds. You can
try and philosophize any which way you want about this
scripture, but there is no getting around what Jesus said. It
doesn't matter who Jesus was talking to or what situation
He was in – take what He said for what it is!

Jesus gave one qualifier to be able to do all the supernatural

extraordinary works that He did. Jesus didn't say you
had to be one of the twelve original apostles, a healing
evangelist, a person in full-time ministry, someone with a
worldwide ministry or a pastor of a ten thousand member
church. Jesus' only qualifier was this: be a believer in Him.
In other words, be a Christian!

For all of the winey, excuse making, cowardly, religious
Christians out there, I'm sure they will find some way to
try and continue to explain themselves out of this. They
will find a way to be a weak, lethargic, good for nothing
"Christian" who sits there and blames God for the lack of
power in the church. Although, there will be a portion of
believers like you and I who will grab hold of what Jesus
said in John 14:12, grab the torch of revival and run with it!
Glory!

You see, in our modern Church, we've gotten so far away
from the true identity of what God made us to be, it's just
flat out ridiculous. Even in the face of scriptures like John
14:12, Christians have made excuses for the lack of power in
their lives and ministries. We've become religious and think
God hasn't given us what we need; so we think we need to
pray, fast and beg for more. We think God is holding out
and so that's why we aren't seeing what we know we should
be seeing.

I want you to think about something. If Jesus said we could
do the same works as Him, don't you think you would need

the same equipment and ability as He had on the earth? It makes sense doesn't it? How can I possibly replicate what Jesus did if I don't have at the very least everything He had? Isn't it ironic that the early Church in the book of Acts didn't pray like Christians pray today? They were aware of what they had and just got the job done. The problem with Christians today is that we don't know what we have. We think we need more power, more anointing, more gifts, more equippings, more this and more that. The reality of the situation is that we have too much!

Friends, we don't have a deficiency problem; we have an awareness problem. I want to show you, as a bona fide believer, what you have on the inside. You my friend are an alien from another planet with superpowers just like Jesus.

> **I keep asking that the God of our Lord Jesus Christ, the glorious Father, may give you the Spirit of wisdom and revelation, so that you may know him better. I pray that the eyes of your heart may be enlightened in order that you may know the hope to which he has called you, the riches of his glorious inheritance in his holy people, and his incomparably great power for us who believe. That power is the same as the mighty strength he exerted when he raised Christ from the dead and seated him at his right hand in the heavenly realms.**
> **Ephesians 1:17-20 NIV**

What was Paul praying? He wasn't praying for God to give

us more. Paul was praying for God to give us revelation so we would understand what we have. Paul knew it wasn't a deficiency problem; it was an awareness problem for the Church.

Did you see what Paul wanted us to be aware of? He wanted us to know three things: God's call on our lives, the riches of our inheritance in Christ and the great power given to us. Great power! And who is that great power for? "...and his incomparably great power for us who believe." Notice just like in John 14:12, the power wasn't for someone with a title or great ministry; the power is for the believer! The only title you will ever need is BELIEVER to do the works of Jesus and manifest the power from your home planet of Heaven.

Also notice the quality of power. It isn't just enough power to heal the sniffles; it's enough power to rock this world. The same power God gave you and I is the same power that raised Jesus from the dead and seated Him at God's right hand! That's some power baby!

If telling us once wasn't good enough, we are told again in Romans 8:11! The same power that God exerted is in us now!

But if the Spirit of Him who raised Jesus from the dead dwells in you, He who raised Christ from the dead will also give life to your mortal bodies through His Spirit who dwells in you.
Romans 8:11 NKJV

For me, this verse ranks right up there with John 14:12. This is an awesome truth and one that should shake you to the core. The same power that raised Jesus from the dead is in you right now! You are not trying to get it; as a believer, you have it - RIGHT NOW! You are a carrier of the power of God. We aren't trying to nag God to give us more; we have it all. The power that produced the greatest act of God for all eternity is bubbling on the inside of you. It's not only there to give life to you now, but also for others. It's like green gobbly goo waiting to ooze out of you! We are aliens from Heaven with supernatural power!

> **Yes, I am the vine; you are the branches. Those who remain in me, and I in them, will produce much fruit. For apart from me you can do nothing.**
> **John 15:5 NLT**

Have you ever seen an apple tree with branches that produced pears? Me neither. You know why? What is flowing through the trunk is flowing through the branches! Jesus is telling us right here that whatever is flowing through Him will be flowing through you. Jesus wants us to produce fruit just like Him.

You can't be in union with Him and not have the same stuff! He is the Head of the Church and we are His body. It's flowing from the top down. Why will we produce much fruit? Because we have everything He had on the earth and even more.

We now have this light shining in our hearts, but we ourselves are like fragile clay jars containing this great treasure. This makes it clear that our great power is from God, not from ourselves.
2 Corinthians 4:7 NLT

Here is another good one. Do you see what the apostle Paul said here? We have a treasure on the inside of us! It's the power of God! He is quick to point out that the great power isn't from us; it's from God. We have alien powers! This demonic doctrine of weak Christianity is just that - demonic. Friend, we are a powerhouse from Heaven! We've been given the same equipment as Jesus so we could perform just like Jesus and have the very same results! You are not lacking in power.

Remember, you are not from here. You may be in this world, but you are not of it. What you see on the outside may tell you that you are weak, but if you'll just look at what's on the inside, you will find that you are strong! This earthly body you have may seem as a fragile clay jar; although, it's not what is on the outside that counts! On the inside of your spirit is the power of Heaven. Inside of you is the Holy Ghost!

And what union can there be between God's temple and idols? For we are the temple of the living God. As God said: "I will live in them and walk among them. I will be their God, and they will be my people."
2 Corinthians 6:16 NLT

> But you belong to God, my dear children. You have already won a victory over those people, because the Spirit who lives in you is greater than the spirit who lives in the world.
> 1 John 4:4 NLT

How can we be weak with God living and dwelling on the inside of us? Do you see how these scriptures blow holes in people's theology of lack? We are asking for God to give us more of Him and yet He, by the Holy Spirit is already in us! If I had an apple in my hand and gave you that apple, wouldn't it be stupid for you to ask me to have more of that same apple? It's just as dumb to ask God for more of Him when He already gave you all of Him! I like something Smith Wigglesworth used to say: "I am a thousand times bigger on the inside than I am on the outside." Why? The Holy Ghost is living in you and living in me!

> I consider that our present sufferings are not worth comparing with the glory that will be revealed in us.
> Romans 8:18 NIV

I like this because it again shows what we have now, not what we are going to have. Notice it doesn't say what will be revealed to us, but what will be revealed in us!
In other words, when we get to Heaven, we will see with unveiled eyes the power and glory of God that was inside of us since we accepted salvation and became new creatures in Christ. For the vast majority of Christians, that will be a sad time; they will realize for the first time who they truly were

in Christ and what He placed in them.

> **In this [union and communion with Him] love is brought to completion and attains perfection with us, that we may have confidence for the day of judgment [with assurance and boldness to face Him], because as He is, so are we in this world.**
> 1 John 4:17 AMP

It doesn't get much better than this. Notice that last phrase: as He is, so are we IN THIS WORLD. This isn't talking about later; it's talking about right now. As Jesus is right now, so are we right now. We won't be like Jesus when we get to Heaven; we are like Jesus right now. The only thing about us that will change is our body. As a man in Christ, our spirit will never change for all of eternity.

You see, we are not in union with the Jesus who walked on the earth. We are in union with the glorified Christ! We are in union with Christ seated at God's right hand. What is flowing through Christ in Heaven is flowing through us on the earth.

We need to know what we have on the inside of us. For too long, we have gone through life as weaklings thinking we couldn't do anything about life's circumstances. But let me tell you something: God has placed the power of Heaven by the Holy Spirit on the inside of you. You have more than enough power to get the job done! You have too much; way too much!

Do you think Jesus is powerless? Do you think Jesus is sitting in Heaven asking God for more power? No! Well then if Jesus isn't, you don't need to either because you are one with Him. You are just like Jesus right here, right now on this earth. You are a supernatural being with supernatural powers! If you need more power, you must not have the Holy Ghost!

Although we don't need more power, you can walk in more and that has everything to do with the renewing of your mind to what you have. It may seem like you need more, but that isn't the case. You simply need to be aware of what you have. The greater your awareness of the power available, the greater power you will see in your life. *We don't have an equipment problem; we have an awareness problem.*

We come from a more powerful Kingdom than the kingdoms of this world. We can get so used to operating in this power that it becomes as natural to us as breathing. The supernatural should be natural to us. It's sad that we have become better at working with electricity than the anointing, but that time is coming to a close.

We are from another world. The more we begin to meditate on who we are and what we possess, the more we will begin to see Heaven on Earth.

CHAPTER SEVEN
THE LAW OF YOUR HOMELAND

For the law of the Spirit of life in Christ Jesus has made me free from the law of sin and death.
Romans 8:2 NKJV

In every country, there are laws that govern that country. There are laws that govern how we treat people, how we drive, how we do business and a host of other types of laws that give us boundaries and govern our lives. With these laws come the authority to enforce them; we see this with judges, politicians, police officers, etc.

During Jesus' earthly ministry, He was operating under the law of Heaven. Even though Jesus lived on the earth, He was living out of Heaven; this is what Jesus meant when He said, "Heaven is where I am from, where I am going and where I am now" in John 3. Jesus was operating with a law of which human nature couldn't understand. It wasn't a physical law, but a spiritual law. It was the law of His homeland.

Jesus understood that the things we see are subject to the

things we can't see; the physical world was birthed out of the spiritual world. Jesus came from a world which had greater power and authority than the world He was temporarily living in.

It is one thing to have power; it is another to have authority to enforce that power. Jesus had both!

> Then Jesus went from village to village, teaching the people. And he called his twelve disciples together and began sending them out two by two, giving them authority to cast out evil spirits.
> Mark 6:6, 7 NLT

Jesus understood it so well that he began to teach the twelve disciples how to work with this Heavenly law. Jesus gave them authority much like a police chief gives authority to his officers to carry out the law of the land.

As the ministry of Jesus began to grow, He needed more ministers, so He appointed seventy more disciples and gave them authority as well (Luke 10). At the end of Jesus' ministry, He enlisted even more disciples and gave us what we know as the Great Commission.

> Jesus came and told his disciples, "I have been given all authority in heaven and on earth. Therefore, go and make disciples of all the nations, baptizing them in the name of the Father and the Son and the Holy Spirit. Teach these new disciples to obey all

**the commands I have given you. And be sure of this:
I am with you always, even to the end of the age."
Matthew 28:18-20 NLT**

In the Great Commission, we see Jesus give all of us the
authority to carry out the laws of Heaven on the earth. It's
interesting to note that Jesus told them He now had all
authority in Heaven and on earth. When Jesus sent out
the twelve and the seventy, He gave them authority. Yet,
after Jesus death, burial and resurrection, Jesus gives us all
authority. Do you see it?

Before Jesus' sacrifice on the cross, He was operating in
a limited authority. Jesus showed us what could actually
be done under the Old Covenant with its limitations.
Although, after Jesus went to hell, soundly defeated Satan
and took the keys of death, hell and the grave, Jesus had all
authority. Once Jesus as the Head of the Church had all
authority, Jesus delegated that authority to us!

In the book of Romans, the apostle Paul sheds light on
the Heavenly law we are to live by; it is the law which
supersedes every limitation that this natural environment
tries to place on us. Remember, we are in the world, but not
of the world - it's a big difference!

**For the law of the Spirit of life in Christ Jesus has
made me free from the law of sin and death.
Romans 8:2 NKJV**

The law of Life is what we operate under. It is the law which we enforce in this earth. You see, when the life you experience on this earth isn't looking much like Heaven, that's where we must rise up and enforce the law of Life. The law of Life is how we can see Heaven on Earth.

We aren't under the rule of Satan anymore. Because of Christ's victory, we went from being Satan's slave to Satan's master! We are no longer subject to the laws of sin and death. Sin, sickness, disease and poverty do not rule over us anymore. The curse which runs rampant on this earth does not have a say over us anymore! The people of this world may be subject to it, but we aren't. We aren't from here!

The laws where we are from supersede the laws of this land. There is a great story about John G. Lake and the law of Life. Lake was a missionary in South Africa in the early 1900's during an outbreak of the Bubonic Plague. During this time, he was out in the fields working with the sick. Several of the doctors who were coming into the area asked Lake how he was able to work with those infected without getting sick. Lake told them to place some of the bacteria on his hand under a microscope. So, the doctors took some of the live bacteria from the inner cheek of the plague's victims and placed it on the palm of Lake's hand. The instant the live bacteria touched Lake's hand, the bacteria died. Lake told the medical professionals that this was the result of the law of Life in Christ Jesus.

You see, although the medical world may give you a death sentence, the law of Life supersedes the laws of this world. You don't have to die when man says you have to die. You don't have to be dominated by life's circumstances; we are to dominate them.

> **Therefore we were buried with Him through baptism into death, that just as Christ was raised from the dead by the glory of the Father, even so we also should walk in newness of life. Likewise you also, reckon yourselves to be dead indeed to sin, but alive to God in Christ Jesus our Lord. For sin shall not have dominion over you, for you are not under law but under grace.**
> **Romans 6:4, 11, 14 NKJV**

The law of sin and death doesn't rule us anymore. This law is what operates in the earth, but again, we are not citizens of this earth; we are citizens of Heaven. This is what should separate us from the citizens of this world; this is what should make us stand out; this is what Jesus was endeavoring to reveal to us during His earth walk.

The law of Life sets us free from our surroundings. Jesus told us how to use this authority in Mark 11:23.

> **For assuredly, I say to you, whoever says to this mountain, 'Be removed and be cast into the sea,' and does not doubt in his heart, but believes that those things he says will be done, he will have whatever he says.**
> **Mark 11:23 NKJV**

Jesus let us know that the law of Heaven superseded where He was currently at. If things needed to change, He changed them. If things need to change in my life, I can change them by enforcing the law of Life in that situation. I can enforce this law because Jesus has sent me from Heaven to manifest Heaven on the Earth.

If things hinder us from doing what God called us to do, then we can change it. If what we are facing goes against what God has provided for us, we can make those circumstances change according to the law of Life. Just like a police officer has a badge, we have a badge. Our badge isn't something we wear, but something we speak. Our badge is the Name of Jesus. It is that Name which allows us to enforce the law of Life! *Jesus is the law of life*

Citizenship Has Advantages

There is a great story found in Acts 22. The apostle Paul had been arrested by the Roman soldiers, but he had a secret: they didn't know he was a Roman citizen.

> The crowd listened to Paul until he said this. Then they raised their voices and shouted, "Rid the earth of him! He's not fit to live!" As they were shouting and throwing off their cloaks and flinging dust into the air, the commander ordered that Paul be taken into the barracks. He directed that he be flogged and interrogated in order to find out why the people were shouting at him like this. As they stretched him

out to flog him, Paul said to the centurion standing there, "Is it legal for you to flog a Roman citizen who hasn't even been found guilty?" When the centurion heard this, he went to the commander and reported it. "What are you going to do?" he asked. "This man is a Roman citizen." The commander went to Paul and asked, "Tell me, are you a Roman citizen?" "Yes, I am," he answered. Then the commander said, "I had to pay a lot of money for my citizenship." "But I was born a citizen," Paul replied. Those who were about to interrogate him withdrew immediately. The commander himself was alarmed when he realized that he had put Paul, a Roman citizen, in chains. The commander wanted to find out exactly why Paul was being accused by the Jews. So the next day he released him and ordered the chief priests and all the members of the Sanhedrin to assemble. Acts 22:22-30 NIV

Notice what happened after the soldiers found out Paul was born a Roman citizen. "Those who were about to interrogate him withdrew immediately. The commander himself was alarmed when he realized that he had put Paul, a Roman citizen, in chains."

This was a serious deal. Roman citizens had rights because of their citizenship. Upon learning of Paul's Roman citizenship, the interrogators got out of there quick and the commander had Paul released. You see, citizenship has advantages. The laws of Rome superseded any other laws in that region. In the same way, the law of Life supersedes the laws of this world.

Sickness, disease, poverty, depression, and addictions must release you when the law of Life is enforced. It is the law of our homeland! It is the law of Heaven! When life's circumstances try to come in and bind you, enforce the law of Life. When the law of Life is enforced with the Name of Jesus, Satan will flee!

Allow this law to operate in every facet of your life. Just because the world says your finances have to be limited, tell the world to shut up! Nothing in my life has to be normal or average. Just because my child is two doesn't mean he has to be terrible. Just because my child is a teenager doesn't mean they have to be rebellious. Just because the world's economy has tanked doesn't mean my finances have to tank. When everything around me is going down, I will keep going up because of the law of Life in Christ Jesus!

We are greater then what the world thinks!

CHAPTER EIGHT
LIVING OUT OF HEAVEN

And yet no one has ever gone up to heaven, but there
is One Who has come down from heaven--the Son
of Man [Himself], Who is (dwells, has His home) in
heaven.
John 3:13 AMP

On the earth, there are some international laws that are
governed and enforced by the United Nations. One law
provides immunity to acting heads of state. Even though
they may be in another country, if while fulfilling their
active duties they commit a crime in that foreign country,
they cannot be held liable while they are actively a head of
state. In other words, they can claim immunity; while an
active head of state, they aren't subject to the laws of the
land because of a higher law.

As aliens on this earth, we aren't subject to the law of sin
and death. We may be in the same surroundings as others,
but the surroundings don't have to have the same effect
on us. In a sense, we are acting heads of state. We are

ambassadors from Heaven appointed, commissioned and sent by Jesus Christ Himself. We are here on the earth conducting government business on behalf of Heaven.

A great example of this is found in Exodus. When you look at the story of how God delivered the Israelites, there are some remarkable truths that apply to us today as Christians. We've all heard about the plagues the Egyptians experienced because Pharaoh wouldn't let the Israelites leave.

A piece of the story we don't think too much about is the fact that the Israelites and Egyptians lived in the same vicinity. While all of the Egyptians were experiencing horrific plagues of locust, frogs, bloody water, etc, these plagues were not affecting the Israelites.

> If you do not let my people go, I will send swarms of flies on you and your officials, on your people and into your houses. The houses of the Egyptians will be full of flies; even the ground will be covered with them. But on that day I will deal differently with the land of Goshen, where my people live; no swarms of flies will be there, so that you will know that I, the LORD, am in this land.
> Exodus 8:21-22 NIV

Isn't that awesome! God was letting them know that even though the land would be full of flies, the Israelites wouldn't experience them. Take special note of verse 23:

And I will put a division and a sign of deliverance between My people and your people. By tomorrow shall this sign be in evidence.
Exodus 8:23 AMP

God actually put a barrier up; you might even say a spiritual force field! The Egyptians and the Israelites were on the same planet in the same country sharing the same ground, but had different results. The Egyptians were trying to survive the circumstances; the Israelites were thriving despite the circumstances! It was not only God showing His faithfulness, love and provision for His people, but also a sign to the Egyptians that there was something different about the Israelites.

So the LORD rained hail on the land of Egypt; hail fell and lightning flashed back and forth. It was the worst storm in all the land of Egypt since it had become a nation. Throughout Egypt hail struck everything in the fields—both people and animals; it beat down everything growing in the fields and stripped every tree. The only place it did not hail was the land of Goshen, where the Israelites were.
Exodus 9:23-26 NIV

Then the LORD said to Moses, "Stretch out your hand toward the sky so that darkness spreads over Egypt—darkness that can be felt." So Moses stretched out his hand toward the sky, and total darkness covered all Egypt for three days. No one could see anyone else or move about for three days.

Yet all the Israelites had light in the places where they lived.
Exodus 10:23-26 NIV

Think about how awesome this was! Where an Egyptian lived, there was darkness; where an Israelite lived, there was light. Wow!   Even though the Egyptians were in total darkness, the Israelites were walking around like nothing had changed.

It is the exact same way for us ambassadors, sent ones, aliens from Heaven. Just like the Israelites, the circumstances of this world do not have to affect us the same way. We have a better covenant with better promises than the Israelites did. How much more should we go through life unaffected by the negative circumstances of this earth?

When Wall Street crashes, when the economy tanks, when everyone else is losing jobs and dying of diseases, when natural disasters strike and the entire world is screaming in terror, we don't have to be affected.

We can keep living life unaffected by disease and poverty. We shouldn't skip a beat! When everything seems like sinking sand, we will still be standing on the rock of Christ! I can be in the world, but not of it; I don't have to allow it to affect me or be in me.

A great example of this in the New Testament is found in Jesus' prayer for us in the Garden of Gethsemane.

> **I have given them Your word; and the world has hated them because they are not of the world, just as I am not of the world. I do not pray that You should take them out of the world, but that You should keep them from the evil one. They are not of the world, just as I am not of the world. Sanctify them by Your truth. Your word is truth.**
> **John 17:14-17 NKJV**

Jesus' prayer was that even though we would be in the world, God would separate us from the evil in this world. Jesus knew that because we were just like Him, we didn't have to experience the same results as the world.

In verse 17, the word sanctify means "to separate or cut out away from." We've been cut out from this world's system. We don't have to live out of the world's economic or health system; we are to live out of Heaven's system! We live according to Heaven's law! Remember what that law is? That's right! It's the law of Life!

Same Conditions; Different Results

I'll never forget a story I heard from a minister about his trip to Haiti. He said he was walking down the streets of Haiti and it was absolute filth. There was trash and raw sewage in the streets and many places didn't have running water; there was simply a devastating poverty in the whole area. He said as they were walking, there was one area of land that caught his attention. There was a mansion sitting on a hill surrounded by lush green grass, perfectly manicured shrubs and trees and enclosed with a large black iron fence and decorative gate at the entrance.

The minister asked his guide whose house it was and the guide said, "That belongs to the ambassador of the United States." Are you getting this? Just because everything around you is in poverty doesn't mean you have to be in poverty. Here was the ambassador from the United States living in wealth while everything around him was in poverty.

The dirt, trash, raw sewage and lack was all around him, but only went up to the borders of his land. The ambassador may have been living in Haiti, but he was living out of the United States. He may have walked the same streets as the Haitians, but he wasn't living like them. His supply source was from his homeland! He didn't have to live like everyone else; he was in that country, but not of it.

Jesus considered Himself a citizen of Heaven and nothing else. Just like the ambassador from the United States, Jesus was living out of another country. Jesus lived out of Heaven! When bills were due, Jesus didn't worry; he could pay his taxes from money found in a fish's mouth (Matthew 17:27) or feed thousands with five loaves of bread and two fish (Matthew 14:19). When leprosy stood right in front of Him and touched Him, the disease didn't get on Jesus - the life in Jesus got on that disease!

I know I am being repetitive, but I am doing it on purpose. We've got to get this. I am in the world, but I am not of it. I may look like everyone else, but I'm not like everyone else. I may be in the same conditions, but I don't have the same results!

> **Since you have been raised to new life with Christ, set your sights on the realities of heaven, where Christ sits in the place of honor at God's right hand. Think about the things of heaven, not the things of earth. For you died to this life, and your real life is hidden with Christ in God.**
> **Colossians 3:1-3 NLT**

Keep your sights on the realities of Heaven. I love that! Keep your focus there and continually think about it. The more you think about the realities of Heaven, the more real it will become to you. You will become increasingly conscious of it and therefore will find it easier to access it! Come on and say it with me, "I am from Heaven. Heaven is my home and I am equipped with the power of Heaven and the authority of Heaven. I am in union with the glorified Christ! What's flowing in Christ is flowing through me. Heaven is where I am from, Heaven is where I am going and Heaven is where I am at right now. I am not of this world!" If that doesn't make you shout, I don't know what will!

CHAPTER NINE
SENT ON A MISSION

For I have come down from heaven not to do my will but to do the will of him who sent me.
John 6:38 NIV

Jesus wasn't sent from Heaven without a purpose; Jesus was sent to this Earth on a mission. He had one priority and that was fulfilling God's will for His life and humanity.

It's important to understand that Jesus understood He was sent for a purpose. He wasn't here to just hang out for 33 years; God always has a purpose behind what He does. Through fellowship with God, Jesus not only found out He was from Heaven but also the reason He was sent.

But he said, "I must proclaim the good news of the kingdom of God to the other towns also, because that is why I was sent."
Luke 4:43 NIV

Just like Jesus, we must understand we are sent ones to this earth. In the book of John alone, Jesus stated "God sent Him" seventeen times. Obviously, if Jesus talked about it that much, then He must have been thinking about it even more. God's mission for His life is what passionately drove Him during His time on the earth.

One of the buzz words around Christianity today is "purpose." Everyone is talking about finding your purpose and fulfilling your purpose. When you understand that you are a sent one, it will help you understand what your purpose is on the earth.

> **For we are God's masterpiece. He has created us anew in Christ Jesus, so we can do the good things he planned for us long ago.**
> **Ephesians 2:10 NLT**

Whether you want to believe it or not, God has a mission for you. Remember what I said earlier? We've been sent here as ambassadors; we are here on a work visa. Our time on the earth is temporary!

Although it is temporary, this time is meant to be used to the fullest in fulfilling God's plan, purpose and pursuit on the Earth. We all have a mission to fulfill. Our tasks and responsibilities may be different, but we all share the same mission. So what is that mission?

Expand the Kingdom Of God

And he called his ten servants, and delivered them ten pounds, and said unto them, Occupy till I come. Luke 19:13 KJV

The word *occupy* means "to conduct business and increase." Friends, God didn't send us here just to sit on our rear ends and do nothing. He didn't send us here to conform to the world; He sent us to transform the world and take over! Remember all the science fiction movies? When the aliens were invading the earth, they weren't coming to make friends and they weren't coming to conform to society. The aliens invaded with the intent to take over.

Well, Jesus has the same mission for you and I. In the story of the talents in Luke 19, the master left the servants for a short time and commanded them to increase his goods while he was gone. Jesus left us the same command; He has commanded us to go into all the world, preach the Gospel of the Kingdom and expand His kingdom upon the earth. It is the will of God!

Read your Bible and you will find out very quickly that God is all about increase! You never find anything small about God; everything is always more than enough, abundant, lavish, excessive, and too much. He is that way with everything including His kingdom.

A major piece of expanding the Kingdom of God included

Jesus equipping others to do the same thing. Basically, Jesus was setting things up and then putting us in charge for a short time until everything was complete; then He would return.

You may say, "How can the kingdom of God increase on the earth?" I'm glad you asked! The kingdom of God can increase in two ways: by number and by influence.

> **He told them, "The harvest is plentiful, but the workers are few. Ask the Lord of the harvest, therefore, to send out workers into his harvest field. Go! I am sending you out like lambs among wolves."** Luke 10:2-3 NIV

Jesus was sent for the harvest. God loves people and He set this whole thing up so His greatest creation could be with Him once again! Once Jesus made the way, He sent us out to continue the mission God gave Him.

Jesus couldn't do it by Himself; He needed more soldiers in the Lord's army. Jesus couldn't go into the entire world by Himself; the world is too big! So, He made a way for the Holy Spirit to reside in each of us so we could take Christ to the world.

God wants His Kingdom full of people; He wants to see the numbers of people in His kingdom go out the roof! First of all, the more people that come to know Jesus as Lord and Savior, the bigger God's Kingdom becomes! God wants

His house full of kids! As the inhabitants of the kingdom increase, so does the number of potential laborers. The more people that are reached for Christ means more people that can preach the good news about Jesus. We must tell people about Jesus!

The second way the kingdom of God can be expanded is by influence. The more aware we become of who we are in Christ and what has been placed in us, the greater influence we will have on the earth. God wants His kingdom to impact every area of our lives as well as those around us.

This is the way we experience true revival! It's not about a program we follow; it is about manifesting the Kingdom of God in such a degree that it begins to ooze out and infiltrate every facet of society including our politics and economics.

You see, it is time for the Christians to take over this planet. We were not sent here to conform to the world; we were sent here to take over! We were sent from Heaven to bring Heaven to this earth and allow others to experience the goodness of God.

Taste and see that the LORD is good.
Psalm 34:8 NIV

For too long we have been telling sinners about the goodness of God and not allowing them to experience it; it's simply because most Christians aren't even experiencing it!

Take a look at the Roman culture during the days of Jesus. Caesar was intent on taking over the world. When the Romans took over - they took over. They not only ruled over that city, but the cultures and everything about that society became conformed to the Roman way of living. It's the same way with God's kingdom. We've been sent on a mission from a country called Heaven to take over in rulership and influence; we are here to rule and reign (Romans 5:17). We are here to dominate, not be dominated.

It's Not Enough to Start The Mission

Completing God's mission was the driving force in the life of Jesus; even in the hard times, the passion to fulfill God's plan kept Him going.
Jesus said to them, "My food is to do the will of Him who sent Me, and to finish His work."
John 4:34 NKJV

Have you ever noticed that when you become extremely hungry, nothing else matters in that moment except finding food? All of a sudden, all the cares and worries of life fade away! Jesus said the food that satisfied Him and sustained Him was not only doing the will of God, but finishing it. There are lots of Christians starting God's plan for their lives and not finishing. It takes determination and fortitude to finish; it takes a love for God and focus on Him to complete your mission. Unfortunately, there are not too many Christians today who are completely sold out to Him;

they are only sold out when it's convenient.

Let me tell you something: if you are on this planet, there will be tough times come your way - Jesus said so. In John 16:33, Jesus said, "In this life you face troubles, but take courage for I have conquered the world." There is a case of "convenient Christianity" that has become an epidemic in the Church.

> **...I do not seek My own will but the will of the Father who sent Me.**
> **John 5:30 NKJV**

For most of modern Christianity, we only serve God when we want to, only go to church when we don't have anything else going on, only give our tithes when we have extra, only bless others when it won't affect our finances, etc. Sadly, many are focused on God's mission as long as it lines up with what we want and it doesn't disrupt our lives.

Most of us get saved and start working on our mission; yet, after some time, we get cold to the things of God, complacent with life and begin to slowly conform to the world instead of transforming the world. We need to keep our "seeker" on God's plan, purpose and pursuits. His mission should be our mission - case closed.

Stay Focused

If we keep our minds focused on the fact that we are sent

from Heaven on a mission, it will always help us keep things in perspective. When life gets tough, you will blow it off because you understand it's just temporary. When circumstances get really bad, it won't faze you because you understand those circumstances can change with just a touch of Heaven.

Always look to Jesus as your example. He's been there and done that! Jesus experienced everything we have and yet still kept His eyes on the prize. Jesus through blood, sweat and tears completed His mission and pleased God; Jesus was faithful to the reason He was sent.

Remember, we are here on this planet for one reason: expand the Kingdom of God. Nothing else in this life matters! We are just here on a work visa; we are here on a business trip so to speak. We are aliens sent to do a job and then leave; it's plain and simple. All you need to do is complete the mission!

Chapter Ten
Alien recognition

34 So now I am giving you a new commandment: Love each other. Just as I have loved you, you should love each other. 35 Your love for one another will prove to the world that you are my disciples."
John 13:34-35 NLT

When you walk into most retail stores, you will notice most businessess enforce a dress code for their employees which usually consists of a uniform. For some of the larger retailers, the uniform their employees wear is almost as recognizable as the logo represnting the company.

One large media and technology retailer's uniform consists of a royal blue shirt and khaki pants. I've seen it so much that when I see someone out in public in a royal blue shirt and khaki pants, I automatically assume they work at this particular business. Why? Because the uniform is recognizable and it sets those individuals apart from others. Their uniform automatically tells me that person works for that company.

In much the same way as a business, Jesus enforced a "uniform" per say for His representatives. Remember I told you we are on a mission from Heaven? We are representatives of Jesus sent into this world to expand the Kingdom of God. You could say we are in the sales business and part of the requirements of working for Jesus is that we are required to wear a uniform.

Now this uniform isn't something made of cotton or polyester. This uniform isn't something you wear on your body. This uniform is an attitude that results in actions. This uniform is that of love.

I know some people who don't like uniforms, but if you want to work for Jesus, this uniform isn't optional. Jesus commanded us to wear it because it will show the world who we are and Who we represent.

Notice Jesus said, "I am giving you a new commandment." Commandments aren't optional; they aren't up for discussion. Commandments are to be obeyed with no questions asked. You don't have to "feel like it" in order to obey a command; all you have to do is - do it.

Jesus also stated in John 13:34,35 the world would know us because of our love for one another. Within this statement, it reveals to us several powerful truths. First of all, we see there are two types of love: God's love and the world's love. Jesus tells us we are to love the way He loves us. How does

Jesus love us? Jesus loves us with a love that has no strings attached. His love doesn't change based on our behavior, His love has no limits and His love isn't based on what I can do for Him. Jesus love for us is so strong and so unselfish that even when we weren't deserving of it and even when we weren't looking for it, Jesus extended His love. The Bible tells us in Romans 5:8 that even while we were still sinners, God demonstrated His love for us by sending Jesus to pay for our sins and sicknesses.

Contrast God's love to the world's love. The world will love you as long as you love them. The world will love you as long as you are a benefit to them. The world will love you in the way you love them. Basically, the world's love is selfish and fickle.

You could liken the world's love to a thermometer and God's love to a thermostat. A thermometer changes with its surroundings; a thermostat stays steady regardless of its surroundings. Jesus wants you to be like a thermostat. Set your love and leave it alone. Don't allow what goes on around you or how people treat you to determine how you will love them. If you do, you start acting like a thermometer and you begin to fluctuate.

So in John 13, we see there are two types of love: God's love and the world's love. Within this passage of scripture is yet another powerful truth: God's love is so strikingly different from the world's love, it will cause you to stand out and be recognizable as one of His own.

So how can we show the world who we are? Love them like Jesus loves us. The world is used to cussing someone out and getting cussed right back. The world is used to yelling at someone and getting yelled at right back. What would happen if someone cussed you out with the nastiest, filthiest language and you didn't respond with hate and contempt? What if you simply smiled back and responded in love? I guarantee they would take notice because it wouldn't be the typical response!

There are a lot of people in the world who claim to be Christians. They proclaim it with their mouth, with the cross hanging around their kneck, their Chistian t-shirt and the fish symbols on their cars - yet I can't tell you how many times I've seen these same people respond to someone publicly with hatred.

There have been countless times I have been driving down the road and been flipped off by someone driving a car with little fishies plastered on the back of their car. What's that all about?

The world isn't stupid. They know counterfeit. They know fake. The sad part is the world has probably seen more fake Christianity than real Christianity. It is a major part of the reason why so many people do not want anything to do with Jesus.

But what if the aliens from Heaven started acting like they were from Heaven? What if we starting truly acting like Jesus instead of the world? What if we started loving the world like Jesus loves us instead of loving the world the way the world loves us?

It's always interesting to me how Christians get mad when people of the world treat them in an unloving way. Don't we realize the world doesn't know any other way to act? It's in their nature and they are going to react and respond the way their daddy, the devil, would react and respond.

So what should our response be? It should be a response of love. Remember, we are to love like Jesus loved us. Jesus love never changes regardless of the way we treat Him; therefore, our love for fellow Christians and for the world should never change regardless of how we are treated.

If we want to truly stand out and be known as disciples of Jesus, it's going to take more than passing out some food or clothes. It's going to come down to character and integrity. How do we as Christians work at our place of employment? Are we prompt in our attendance? Are we constantly late? Are we always calling in sick? Do we go over and beyond the call of duty or do we do just enough to get by?

What about out in public? How do we treat the waitstaff in a restaurant? How do we treat the police officer that pulled us over because we were speeding? How do we treat the neighbors in our neighborhood? Do we love these people or do we talk down to them?

You see, it is in these types of situations where the world will take notice. The world expects churches to do nice things in the community, but when it comes down to individual Christians - you never know what you are going to get! The people you are around on a daily basis are watching you. The more you advertise yourself as a Christian, your actions will result in either pulling people to Jesus or pushing them away. Your love toward others will make you recognizable as an authentic legit follower of Christ or some cheap knock off.

Jesus has sent us on a mission to reach the world, but no one is going to pay attention to us and recognize us as His until we put on our uniform. It is the uniform that sets you apart and proves that you are truly a representative of Jesus. It's one thing to be sent by Jesus; it's another to be recognized as one sent by Jesus. Get recognized!

CHAPTER ELEVEN
PLEASE GOD, NOT PEOPLE

And He who sent Me is with Me. The Father has not left Me alone, for I always do those things that please Him.
John 8:29 NKJV

We all have a natural, innate tendency to want people to like us; although, too many times, we allow this to hinder us in completing God's mission on the earth. When you are so focused on being liked, you will begin to slowly stop doing what God has called you to do and saying what God has called you to say.

For fear of criticism and lack of popularity, even ministers today are backing off the Truth of God's Word. Pastors are watering down the Message to fill the pew; they back off of the moving of the Holy Spirit because they don't want to offend anyone. It's funny to me that Jesus wasn't like that. Jesus just flat out told it like it was and He moved whenever the Holy Spirit wanted. He told the religious leaders to their faces that their daddy was the devil and they were from hell and healed people on the Sabbath knowing the Pharisees would be mad!

Jesus was not well liked during His time. The religious people hated Him. Most people only wanted to be around Him so they could get their needs met. Jesus was talked about left and right, up and down and all the way around.

If the printing press would have been invented, people would have written books about Him just to bash Him. If television would have been around, reporters would have been there to criticize him and many of the television evangelists of the day would have been calling Him the devil. Let me put it to you like this: if everyone likes you, you've got a serious problem. More than likely, it is a very good indicator that you are a people pleaser and not a God pleaser.

You might as well understand it now. The more you begin to look like Jesus, live like Jesus and act like Jesus, the more you will begin to be treated like Jesus. Remember, we have different laws that we live by, a different language that we speak and different powers with which we operate. Aliens are different; they stick out.

People like to make fun of differences. Remember when you were in school? The kids that didn't dress like the other kids were made fun of and kids with funny names or accents were ridiculed. If you are living like an alien from

Heaven, there will be qualities that simply separate you from everyone else around you.

> **Not with eyeservice, as men-pleasers, but as bondservants of Christ, doing the will of God from the heart, with goodwill doing service, as to the Lord, and not to men.**
> **Ephesians 6:6-7 NKJV**

Don't worry about pleasing the people around you. When they make fun of you for talking about how healed you are even though it's obvious you don't feel well - so what! When you are criticized for praising God that you are rich even though you may not have the money in the bank to pay the light bill - so what! When people laugh at you when you declare God's promises of provision and protection in the face of adversity - so what! Jesus never cared and you should not care either! Remember, the people jeered and laughed at Jesus when He spoke the language of Faith; if they mocked Jesus, they will mock you.

When the world and even other Christians criticize you, don't worry about it. Let them talk the language of fear and keep living their life of misery and despair. I am a citizen of Heaven, an alien of another World and I speak the language of Faith regardless of what people say. Because you know what? They won't be laughing when they see my body resurrected. They won't be jeering when they see me with way too much money. They won't be criticizing when they come to me for help! They won't be mocking me when their world looks like Egypt and my world looks like Goshen!

> **For do I now persuade men, or God? Or do I seek to please men? For if I still pleased men, I would not be a bondservant of Christ.**
> **Galatians 1:10 NKJV**

You were not sent from Heaven to be liked on the earth. You were sent on a mission. You are different - get over it. To the world, you look different, dress different, smell different, sound different and act different. You will be made fun of and you will be mocked. It's called suffering for Jesus and it is simply part of the Christian life.

Now please don't misunderstand me; I'm not saying be mean to people. We need to love people like Jesus loves people, but true love speaks truth. We are to honor people, respect people and love people, but we are not to cower down to their opinions and disbeliefs about God and His Word. We are not to back off of the power of God and the moving of the Holy Spirit just because it scares the religious people of the day. We are not to back off of preaching the truth of God's Word simply because you are being labeled as preaching hate.

In the society we live in, the criticisms are only going to get worse. Have you looked at television lately? Anytime a Christian stands up for morals and family values, they are trashed for being intolerant and spewing hate speech by the liberal media. A Christian stands up against abortion and homosexual marriages and they are labeled as a hate monger.

Personally, I have received letters and emails telling me I'm going to hell for what I am preaching. I've had Christians tell me I'm being mean to people because I'm getting their hopes up in the area of healing. Well, they are right about getting their hopes up; that is my whole intent. When you give people the Word, it cause faith and hope to rise up and that is when the miracles begin!

Let me tell you something: I'm focused on one thing and that is doing what God sent me to do. I don't care what people think about me or say about me; I really truly don't. I have taken on the attitude of Jesus: I will do what pleases God despite what man says or does to me.

I'm not concerned with winning man's popularity contest because I wasn't sent to this earth to win a pageant. I wasn't sent from Heaven to see how many Facebook friends I can acquire or how many people I can get into a church service. The one reason I was sent was to do God's mission for my life and thus do that which pleases Him - complete it.

CHAPTER TWELVE
YOU ARE NOT ALONE

And He who sent Me is with Me. The Father has not left Me alone...
John 8:29 NKJV

One of the secrets to Jesus' success is found here in John 8:29; Jesus was aware of the presence of God. Like I said earlier, in this life, there will be some hard times. There will be some rough patches you will go through and some negative circumstances that come your way. Regardless of what occurs, always know that you are never alone.

There will be plenty of times in life when Satan will try to make you think you are out there all by yourself. It will be in these times you will be tempted to quit and give up. You will be tempted to abandon the mission and abandon your true identity because of people and life's circumstances. But realize what Jesus said, "He who sent me is with me."

Even though you've been sent from Heaven, God still came with you. When you are facing a really bad situation, always remember that God is there. Everywhere you go,

God is there because you are the temple of the Holy Spirit; you are a carrier and vessel of God (1 Corinthians 3:16.)

Yet, it's not enough to simply be aware of God's indwelling presence; you need to be aware of His manifest presence. There is a level of fellowship with God where you can actually feel Him and hear Him. This is where Jesus was in His walk with God and it should be where we are as well.

When you know that God is with you and I mean you know that you know - nothing will ever take away your focus. There will be nothing that will ever take you off your mission. There will be no person, no amount of fame, fortune or success that will sway you from doing what God has sent you to do. You will never be afraid and never doubt. You will never wonder if the victory is yours. You will never wonder if you can do what God called you to do. When you know God is with you, when you are aware of His manifest presence - nothing will ever stand in your way.

Regardless of how hard the mission may seem, there will be nothing you can't accomplish because God is there. Because He is with us and in us, we don't have to complete His mission in our own strength; we are to use all that He is! We use His faith, His power, His peace, His joy and His victory. We can never fail when we know, just like Jesus, our Father is with us.

Chapter Thirteen
Return Of the Mothership

**For the Lord himself will come down from heaven,
with a loud command, with the voice of the
archangel and with the trumpet call of God, and the
dead in Christ will rise first. After that, we who are
still alive and are left will be caught up together with
them in the clouds to meet the Lord in the air. And
so we will be with the Lord forever.**
1 Thessalonians 4:16-17 NIV

Whether people want to believe it or not, Jesus is coming
back. The Head of the Church is coming back for His
Church; the Commander of God's army is coming back for
His troops; the mothership will return for its aliens.

We were not sent from Heaven, dropped off, abandoned
and left here forever. Remember our time here is
temporary; we were simply sent here on a mission.

God sent you here on a business trip. I keep using the
comparison of a work visa because it has so much truth to

it. With a work visa, you are allowed into a country for a short period of time and then you are required to go back to your country of origin. The same thing applies to us as aliens from Heaven. We've been sent to the earth to conduct business and occupy the land until Jesus comes back for us.

> **And he called his ten servants, and delivered them ten pounds, and said unto them, Occupy till I come. Luke 19:13 KJV**

You haven't been left alone and you haven't been left for good either! Jesus is coming back. You see, we can say just like Jesus did in John 3:13:

> **And yet no one has ever gone up to heaven, but there is One Who has come down from heaven--the Son of Man [Himself], Who is (dwells, has His home) in heaven.**
> **John 3:13 AMP**

Heaven is where I am from and Heaven is where I am going! We need to get excited about this. Keeping this truth in the forefront of your mind will help you. Not only can you take courage that God is with you, but you can also take solace in the truth that you won't be here long!

Our homeland is so much better than where we are now; Heaven makes Hawaii look like a dump! The scenery is better, the lifestyle is better and even the food is better!

Watching The Clock Count Down

I don't know about you, but when I am exercising, it always helps me to look at the clock. If I have a specific amount of time that I am running, it helps me to see how much time I have left - it basically helps me to keep my sights on the end. As a result, I am better able to focus on the end and push myself to finish.

> **Therefore keep watch, because you do not know on what day your Lord will come.**
> **Matthew 24:42 NIV**

Although we do not know the specific day and time of Jesus' return, we are given many clues as to roughly when this will occur. Without getting into all the scriptures which reveal these clues, I'll just say for me personally, I believe it will be very soon.

> **But understand this: If the owner of the house had known at what time of night the thief was coming, he would have kept watch and would not have let his house be broken into. So you also must be ready, because the Son of Man will come at an hour when you do not expect him.**
> **Matthew 24:43-44 NIV**

Just because we don't know the day and time, we don't have to be clueless. Jesus said if we don't watch, it will be to us as a thief breaking into our house at night. This tells me that if we are expecting, if we are watching, we don't have to be caught surprised at His coming.

> **Who then is the faithful and wise servant, whom the master has put in charge of the servants in his household to give them their food at the proper time? It will be good for that servant whose master finds him doing so when he returns. Truly I tell you, he will put him in charge of all his possessions. But suppose that servant is wicked and says to himself, 'My master is staying away a long time,' and he then begins to beat his fellow servants and to eat and drink with drunkards. The master of that servant will come on a day when he does not expect him and at an hour he is not aware of. He will cut him to pieces and assign him a place with the hypocrites, where there will be weeping and gnashing of teeth.**
> Matthew 24:45-51 NIV

Do you see the importance of watching and expecting His return? It will keep us focused on our mission. It will keep us focused on pleasing Him and not pleasing people. It will keep us from getting lazy and cold to the things of God; we won't begin conforming to the world.

The Christians we see today who live like the world, talk like the world and look like the world - they live like this because they aren't looking for the return of Jesus. They are not watching for Him; otherwise, they would start living for Him and doing what He said to do.

I know everyone of us at some point in time at our jobs have acted the way Jesus described with these servants. When we knew the boss was going to be away for a few days, we started to slack off on our work, maybe came in late and left early and basically just acted in ways we normally wouldn't have. If the boss left the office and didn't give us an exact time of their return, we were less likely to slack off in our work. Why? You didn't want to get caught!

Well, I don't want to get caught not fulfilling my mission. When Jesus returns, I won't be totally surprised because I will be watching for Him. We should live every day like it is the day Jesus is returning. We should live every hour like it is the last one we have on the earth for Jesus. *We should live every moment like it is the last time to bring someone else into the Kingdom of God!* Contrary to what is being preached today, there is a literal Hell and a literal Heaven. There is very much a Hell to shun and a Heaven to gain!

Jesus is coming soon my friend. You and I, along with all of our fellow brother and sisters in Christ, are going back to our homeland very soon. We will hear that trumpet sound, see the Heavens open up and rise to meet Jesus in that great cloud of glory. Heaven is where I am from and it's where I am going back to very soon!

Closing

Always remember who you truly are; you are not what you see in the mirror. Your identity is found in Christ.

Always remember what you truly have. You are not lacking in any way. You are not deficient. You have the life and nature of God in you.

Stay focused on God. Fellowship with Him and maintain an awareness of His presence in your life.

Don't worry about people's opinions. The people who try to pull you down and keep you back won't be standing with you when you give an account before Jesus of what you did for Him on the earth.

Make completing God's mission the driving force in your life. Make it your goal to take as many people back to Heaven as possible. Watch expectantly for Jesus' return.

Heaven is where we are from. Heaven is where we live out of and Heaven is where we are going!

God bless you my friend. In Him, we always win!

Prayer For Salvation And The Baptism Of The Holy Spirit

Dear friend, it is the desire of God that everyone accepts His free gift of salvation. God sent the greatest gift Heaven had so the world could be set free; that precious gift was Jesus! Despite knowing the mistakes you would make, He died for you anyway. Jesus knew the sins you would commit, yet He still climbed up on the cross. Why? *His love was greater than your sin.*

Romans 10:9, 10 says if you will confess Jesus as your Lord and Savior and believe that He arose from the dead, you will be saved. You see, salvation has nothing to do with works. It doesn't matter what church you belong to, how many little old ladies you help across the street or how much you give the church. You cannot earn salvation; you cannot buy salvation; you must simply accept salvation.

Another free gift that God has provided is the Baptism of the Holy Spirit. In Acts 2, we find the Baptism of the Holy Spirit being given to the Church. God desires that you be filled with His Spirit with the evidence of speaking in tongues.

God said in Acts 2:38 that this life changing gift was for everyone, not just a select few. It wasn't just for those living in Bible days; it was given to everyone who would accept Jesus as Lord and Savior. Jesus said the purpose of the Bap-tism of the Holy Spirit was so you could be a witness! You'll find that when you receive the Baptism of the Holy Spirit, it allows you to operate in the fullness of God's power and be a blessing to the entire world.

Regardless of who you are, God has a plan for your life. He wants you to be successful, have all your needs met and live a life of victory. God wants every day of your life to be a day full of peace and joy, but it all begins with Jesus being your Lord. If you have never accepted Jesus as your Lord and Savior, please pray this prayer with me right now:

Jesus, I confess that I am a sinner. I realize I can't do this on my own. I believe with my heart and confess with my mouth that you died on the cross for my sins and sicknesses and arose from the dead. I ask you to be the Lord and Savior of my life. I thank you for forgiving me of my sins and loving me enough to give your life for me. I thank you that I am now a child of God! I now ask you for the infilling of the Holy Spirit. You said in Your Word that it was a free gift so I receive it now. I thank you for my Heavenly prayer language!

We encourage you to become involved in a solid Bible based church; if you need help finding a church in your area, contact us through the information below.

Begin reading your Bible and praying in the Spirit daily. Now it is time to start developing your relationship with your Heavenly Father and growing in the Lord. Don't forget to tell someone about what Jesus did for you! Remember that God is good and He has good things in store for you!

If you prayed this prayer, would like assistance in locating a local church or this book has impacted your life, we would love to hear from you! You can also obtain a full listing of our books, CD's, DVD's and other teaching materials by contacting us at:

www.ChadGonzales.com

About The Author

Chad and Lacy are on a mission to reveal God's goodness, His love and His power in these final days. It is their heart for all people to know who they truly are in Christ and all that He has provided for them.

With a strong emphasis on one's identity in Christ, healing and the ministry of the Holy Spirit, they declare the Word of God with great boldness and without compromise. As a result, miraculous healings are common in their ministry including blind eyes and deaf ears healed, tumors dissolved, chronic diseases healed and many more.

CPSIA information can be obtained
at www.ICGtesting.com
Printed in the USA
FSHW022358270919
62453FS